Dog

Owner's Manual

Important Stuff You Should Know About Your Pet

By Buster
As Told to David E. Carter

Andrews McMeel Publishing

Kansas City

ISBN: 0-7407-1042-7

Library of Congress Catalog Card Number: 00-108473

ATTENTION: SCHOOLS AND BUSINESSES

Andrews McMeel books are available at quantity discounts with bulk purchase for educational, business, or sales promotional use. For information, please write to: Special Sales Department, Andrews McMeel Publishing, 4520 Main Street, Kansas City, Missouri 64111.

This book is dedicated to Trixie, King, Lady, Lowley,
and, most of all,
Buster.

You all gave us much more than we could ever give you.

People know so little about what goes on inside the minds of dogs.

This book should help.

Topics included in this manual:

- Favorite dog fantasies
- Dog behavior (inside the canine mind)
- Dog language
- If dogs ran things...
- Dog unsolved mysteries
- Dog letters
- Little-known facts about dogs
- And a lot more...

The Dog National Anthem

While I lie here slee—ping
getting rubbed on the ear,
I give thanks for my home
and the people who live here.

Cats may have kitty lit—ter,
and beds made from velvet rags,
but only in the U.S.
do they have doggy bags.

Forget about breeds.

To dogs, there are only three kinds of other dogs:
- Dogs bigger than I am, whom I greatly respect
- Dogs my size
- Small dogs I can intimidate

CLASS

Dogs are very
class conscious.
There are two social
classes of dogs:
- Outside dogs
- Inside dogs

(There are some bi-side dogs who "go both ways.")

Outside dogs
    really resent
        inside dogs.

Especially when it's cold and rainy.

Lame Excuse at
Dog Obedience School:

My person
ate my
homework.

3 Theories on Why Dogs Howl:

1. It's how dogs clear their throats.

2. Dog translation means "I'm really bored."

3. It's a sign of dog PMS.

Favorite Dog Fantasy #545:

This guy who lives in my house is cooking six big steaks on the grill. But he starts telling a joke, and he forgets what he's doing. Then he notices that he has burned the steaks so that people don't want them. And then he yells "C'mere Buster."

If dogs ran things...

Fleas would be as big as frogs, and taste like raw hamburger.

If Rembrandt had been a dog,

<u>this</u> would have
certainly been his
greatest work.

If dogs ran things . . .

Pizza would come in "dirty sneakers" flavor.

Why dogs are more fun
on car trips than kids:

1. Dogs never have sticky fingers from eating candy.

2. Dogs don't want to stop at every McDonald's.

3. Dogs never say "when will we be there?"

Favorite Dog Fantasy #521:

The people who live in my house are gone, and I walk down the hall to the Oasis, and I find that

someone made
blue Kool-Aid
just for me!

If dogs ran things ...

Baths would be OPTIONAL.

"Sniffing" other dogs is actually governed by very strict rules of dog etiquette.

If dogs ran things...

There would be a cat fight on HBO every night.

Well-kept secret about dogs:

Some very small dogs are actually cats in drag.

(That's just one reason why dogs "sniff.")

Why dogs can't stop
at just <u>any</u> tree.

What you see —

What dogs see—

Why dogs can't type:

The quick brown fox jumped ovrr
the lazy sleeping dog.
The click brown fox jumped over
the lazy sleeping dog.
The quicg brown fox jumped over
the lazy bleeping dog.

Dogs refuse to write words
that demean their own
species.

If dogs ran things...

Leashes would be
just a little longer.

Better still, leashes
would be ILLEGAL.

Really Bad Dog Nightmare #1:

The blind date

Male   Female

Favorite Dog Fantasy #31:

The guy who lives in my house is reading a book, and I quietly go over and sit beside him. Without even thinking about it, he begins to rub my stomach. I close my eyes and quickly doze off. He keeps rubbing me, even as I sleep.

Favorite dog pick-up line (male to female):

I've been fixed. I swear.

Favorite dog pick-up line (female to male):

Little-known facts about dogs:

Dog "singles bars" are very popular.

Typical night at "Heat,"
a popular hangout in season.

Favorite Dog Fantasy #44:

This famous film producer comes to my door and says, "Hollywood has a need for a dalmatian with your obvious class, looks, and charm.

"Would you like to star in a big MOVIE?"

Favorite Dog Fantasy #45:

So, I become a big star.

And I get invited to this
late-night talk show,
where I get to read
the "Top Ten Reasons
Why Dogs Are Better
Than Cats."

"Top Ten Reasons Why Dogs Are Better Than Cats."

10. Litter boxes.
9. Try calling a cat. Say "here kitty" and watch what happens. Nothing.
8. Cats spray. Who do they think they are, anyway?
7. They won't eat table scraps.

6. That silly "purring" gets on a guy's nerves.
5. Cats have tongues like sandpaper.
4. They have whiny little voices.
3. Cats have fish breath.
2. Cats are always licking themselves.
1. They don't even know <u>where</u> to lick.

If dogs ran things...

Mount Rushmore would include at least one dog.

Maybe
TWO.

Really Bad Dog Nightmare #2:

You sniff a really huge dog in a friendly way, and then you remember the smell — a long time ago, when the other dog was just a pup, you chased him away from your place. And he suddenly remembers who you are . . .

If you see your dog "running" while asleep, this is most likely what he's dreaming.

Dog magic secret revealed:

What the
audience
sees —

How they
do it –

Q.

Why do dogs chase cats?

A. It's actually a game.
The cat pretends to be a speeding driver, and the dog is the sheriff.

A letter to the people who make tennis balls:

Dear people who make tennis balls,

Dogs love tennis balls.
They're just the right size.

But you should do something about that fuzz on the outside. When it gets wet, it smells like a wet person. Maybe you could change the flavor of the fuzz . . .

P.S. I think hamburger
flavor might be good.

Or how about road-kill possum?

Favorite Dog Fantasy #107:

So I'm out for a walk with this guy
I own, and we see this great-looking bitch.

I say, "I love
the smell of
your perfume, baby."

And she says, "Your place or mine?"

Then I notice that my guy isn't holding the leash very tightly.

And then I'm gone for about two days.

How people give directions:

Go three blocks, until you come to a red light.
Turn right. Go two blocks,
and turn left on Rhodes.

Next, go on the road until
you see a gas station on
the left. Turn there, and
then look for the second
house on the left. The porch light will be on for you.

How dogs give directions:

Go down that path that has the cat smell, until
you come to a robin's nest
in the tree. Turn right.

Then go past the old
place where the junkyard
dog lives. But go fast.
Then look for the dog with a
spot on his eye. I live next door. Inside.

If dogs ran things...

The top movie of all time
would have been directed by
STEVEN SPEILBARK,
an all-animal film...

about dinosaurs and hogs ... called

JURASSIC PORK.

Favorite Dog Fantasy #747:

I'm out by myself for a walk, minding my own business. Along comes this dog catcher, and he thinks I should be a "pound dog." He starts to chase me, and I'm running at about half speed ...

and about that time, he makes a big lunge
at me. And that's when I really turn on
the burners. Why, by the time his net
hits the ground, I'm several feet
away. And the guy hits with a
thud and says, "*@#%*&>* dog."

Did you ever see a dog smile?

If dogs ran things...

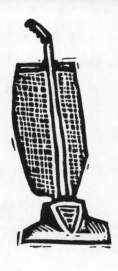

Vacuum cleaners would NOT be allowed around food on the floor.

Only DOGS would be allowed to pick up dropped food — no matter how small the serving.

If dogs ran things...

And while we're talking about food — no plate would be allowed in the sink or dishwasher unless it was first LICKED CLEAN by the dog of the house.

Failure to obey this law would be punishable by a mandatory "ear scratch" accompanied by the words "good dog."

Little-known fact about dogs:

Dogs are environmentalists.

Pop-Quiz Question at Dog Obedience School:

If people turn in "dog-eared" papers what do dogs do with <u>their</u> papers?

If dogs ran things . . .

They'd change the face of the Sphinx . . .

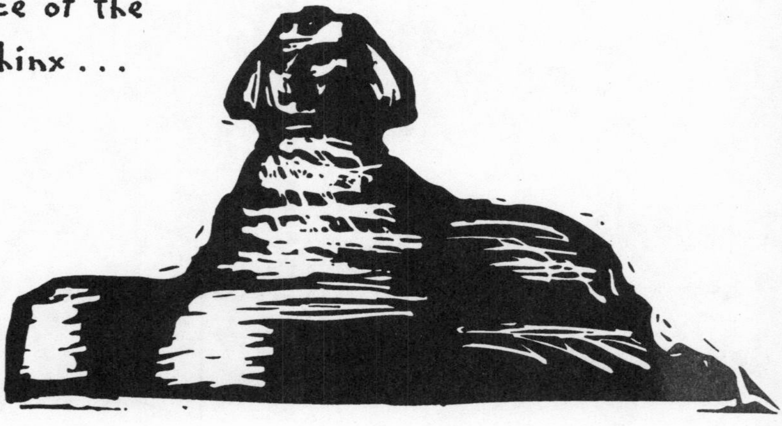

and make it PRETTIER.

Why dogs don't like coffee:

1. Keeps them awake during the day.

2. Dogs don't do spoons very well.

3. "Oasis water" is much better.

Favorite Dog Universities

University of Georgia
(BULLDOGS)

Southern Illinois University
(SALUKIS)

Mantz State
(MONGRELS)*

*Not really. But maybe someday.

Why male dogs don't wear boxer shorts:

1. They don't match the coat.

2. Where would the tail go?

3. Interferes with sniffing.

Thousands of farmers
would grow a crop called
"Table Scraps."

Secret Dog Slang

Dog Days:

traditional summertime
group activity;
also called the
"sniffing festival."

Favorite Dog Fantasy #406:

This kid who lives next door sees me outside and comes over with a stick in his hand. He throws it about one hundred feet away and says, "Fetch."

I look at him, and in a deep voice, say, "Fetch it yourself, kid."

If dogs ran things...

Food bowls would be measured by the gallon, and there would be unlimited refills.

Why female dogs
don't wear bikinis:

If dogs ran things...

The dollar (\$) would be replaced by the bone (B).

And Buster would be on the Ƀ5 bill.

What big dogs
think about
little dogs
(and vice versa):

Report Card from Obedience School

Roll Over	B
Sit	A-
Stay	A
Beg	A+
Fetch	B-

Remarks

Sniffs others
improperly

If dogs ran things ...

Frisbee catching would be a major league sport.

And the best dogs would make a lot of ₿.

Secret Dog Slang

Dog Fashion:

to be nattily
attired and
well groomed*

*A requirement to successfully take part in the Heat Festival.

Another reason why dogs are better than cats:

Cats bring you unwanted "presents."

Why don't they just learn how
to dig holes and <u>bury</u> stuff?

Why dogs don't like bowling:

1. There's no way to get a bowling ball in your mouth.

2. The ball comes back to you automatically. That's <u>dog</u> work.

3. All those "pins" used to be trees. (Dogs NEED trees.)

Why dogs chase cars:

1. Deep Freudian compulsion: The dog is thinking, "Is my mother in that car?"

2. Legend has it that there are five female dogs in the backseat, and if you catch the car ... never mind — dogs never catch cars.

3. Revenge motive — "a car something like that hit my best friend."

Dog Law 101 — Dog Negotiation

1. Whoever growls louder — wins.
2. If the little dog growls louder,
   negotiations are over, and
   the dog fight begins.

Secret Dog Slang

Doggone:

commonly used by people
as a softer expletive, as
in "doggone, that hurt."

As used by dogs, refers
to missing canine.

Why dogs aren't welcome at Wimbledon:

The world's top players haven't learned how to play with a ball that's loaded with dog saliva.

Dogs would have their own paths.

Why there are no
famous dog singers:

1. Dogs have a very limited octave range.

2. Without pockets, dogs find it very difficult to buy CDs.

3. The best composers don't understand the language.

Why do people show their teeth when they're happy? Why don't they just wag their tail, the way they're supposed to?

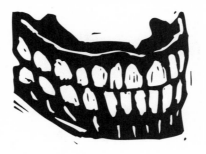

Why do some people take out part of their face, and then put it in a glass of water? And then they don't even drink the water.

Daily Schedule: Active Dog

8:00   Eat
9:00   Walk to the tree
9:30   Nap
12:00 Bark at mailman
12:05 Nap
6:00   Eat
7:00   Walk to tree
8:00   Bedtime

Daily Schedule: Retired Dog

8:00   Eat
9:00   Walk to the tree
9:30   Nap
12:00 Mailman disturbs sleep
12:05 Back to sleep
6:00   Eat
7:00   Walk to tree
8:00   Bedtime

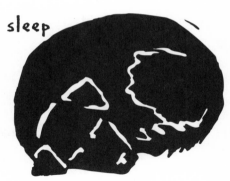

Letter to the people who make hot dogs:

Dear people who make hot dogs,

Don't get me wrong.
Dogs love hot dogs.

But couldn't you call them something else?
Why take a chance on giving people ideas?
How about calling them ... HOT CATS?

Favorite Dog Fantasy #606:

Dog Wins Nobel Prize
for Friendship to Man

Why dogs love classical music:
The best violins use
CAT GUT for strings.

Things that dogs think are
really stupid:

Cats playing with yarn
is really stupid.

In fact, cats are
really stupid.

What dogs do when no one takes them for a ride.

Great Dog Moment #77:

The people forget to buy dog food and have to feed me TABLE SCRAPS.

How to have a great dog party:

Have lots of cat piñatas
and fill them with
raw hamburger.

Doghouses would
be a LOT bigger.

Dog Profanity:

To most dogs,
BATH is a
four-letter word.

Things dogs have in common with people:

Both hate to wait in line
for the rest room.

Why dogs don't
celebrate holidays:

They're frankly a bit miffed that cats have Halloween and rabbits have Easter. And . . . dogs have NOTHING.

Small pleasures in a dog's life:

Watching the people go out for
a few hours and finding
that the garbage can is
full and the lid is loose.

If dogs ran things...

Rolling in the floor
to scratch your back
would be a "gymnastics
for dogs" event in
the Olympics.

Why dogs have fast mood changes:

The dog gets territorial and is really barking a lot, chasing away another dog on his turf.

Suddenly, he sees just how BIG the other dog really is . . .

The dog quickly thinks things over and decides that this would be a perfect time to scratch for fleas, or take a nap.

Dogs mood changes (continued):

The big dog keeps coming, and the formerly barking dog realizes that he is in trouble. "This might be a good time to go into my doghouse," the dog thinks. "The one with a very small door."

f you enjoyed this book:

1. Give your inside dog an extra snack.
2. Let your outside dog come in for a while.
3. Take a minute to realize just how much your dog means to you.

Thanks for reading my book. Buster.

Book production notes:

The neat art in this book is just a small sample
of the computer clip art that is available from
two crazy and talented guys named Ron and Joe.
So it's appropriate that we include this line:
Illustrations © 2000 by Art Parts/Ron & Joe, Inc.
For more product information: www.ronandjoe.com.

Also, the type used throughout this book is called
Regular Joe, and is also the work of Ron and Joe.
(These are the only products endorsed by Buster.)